101
Things a College Girl Should Know
From a Big Sister Who's Been There

101

Things a College Girl Should Know
From a Big Sister Who's Been There

STEPHANIE EDWARDS

Andrews and McMeel
A Universal Press Syndicate Company
Kansas City

For information write to Andrews and McMeel, a Universal Press Syndicate Company,
4520 Main Street, Kansas City, Missouri 64111.

Library of Congress Cataloging-in-Publication Data
Edwards, Stephanie, 1971-
   101 things a college girl should know, from a big sister who's been there / Stephanie
Edwards.
      p. cm.
   ISBN 0-8362-1090-5 (pbk)
   1. College student orientation—United States. 2. Women college students—United
States—Conduct of life. 1. Title.
LB2343.32.E363 1996
378.19'81—dc20   95-50502
                                                                   CIP

03 04 COM 10 9

Attention: Schools and Businesses
Andrews and McMeel books are available at quantity discounts with bulk
purchase for educational, business, or sales promotional use.
For information, please write to
Special Sales Department, Andrews and McMeel, 4520 Main Street,
Kansas City, Missouri 64111.

Amy,

I hope this little guide is helpful to you. I tried to think of all the things I wish I'd known when I was a freshman. This list is advice based on some of the things I did wrong, some of the things I saw my friends do wrong, and some of the things that all first-year students (and some fifth-year students) do wrong. I hope you can learn from our mistakes.

Good luck! I love you and wish you all the best. If you ever have any questions, remember you can always ask me. After all, that's what smarter and wiser big sisses are for. . . .

Love,
Steph

1

*Always drink eight glasses
of water a day.*

2

*Whenever a professor offers
office hours, visit him / her.*
It makes a good impression.

3
Save money the summer before you go away to school.
Parents never give you enough money.

4
Don't get drunk and order pizza.
It costs a lot and you'll put on the lbs.

5
Learn the library
IMMEDIATELY!!!

6

*Join whatever clubs
you have time for.*

7

*Write for the school paper
or literary magazine.*

8

Make yourself floss every day.

9

Take one of the free courses offered (karate, tennis, etc.) at the school gym or recreation center.

10

If grandparents are looking for a way to help you out, ask for rolls of quarters.

They are a necessity for doing laundry.

11

Never take the elevators on campus.
Stairs are the best!

12

*Bring lots of pictures from home
for your dorm room.*

13
Take many pairs of underwear with you.

14
Bring a laundry bag.

15
Begin budgeting yourself the minute you arrive.

16
Don't miss on-campus meals.

17

In the cafeteria, take extra fruit for later.

AVOID THE VENDING MACHINES.

18

Never walk alone at night.

19
Remember:
Frat guys + beer = TROUBLE

20
Don't get a reputation;
they're easy to gain and hard to lose.

21

*Go to the
"Take Back the Night" rally.*

22

*Study at coffee shops with funky
names that play interesting music.*

23

Only pack clothes you've worn in the past six months.

If you think you won't need it ... you won't!

24

Buy a used bike with an unbreakable lock.

Graduating seniors always sell bikes – check the bulletin boards.

25
Save the boxes you shipped your stuff to school in.

26
Don't buy notebooks in the university bookstore ($$$).

27
Always lock your dorm room.
Your next-door neighbor could be a recovering klepto.

28
Have a durable backpack with your name on it.

29
Buy a school sweatshirt.
You'll wear it the rest of your life.

30
Read a novel every month.
It can be short and trashy – just read for pleasure.

31
Hold office in the student government, a sorority, or a club.

32
*Have friends of many different races,
persuasions, and religions.*

33
TALK, TALK, TALK *in class.*
Many classes need the female viewpoint.

34
Tutor challenged kids after school.

35
*Help with the
school recycling program*
or start one.

36
Write ALL *assignments down.*
If not, you'll always forget one.

37
Read what is assigned.
It helps immensely at exam time.

38
Read what is assigned
even if the professor doesn't call on students.

39
Read ahead!

40
Get a date book and record all long-term assignments on syllabus day.

41

Schedule your classes early in the morning or all in the afternoon.

42

Don't start the weekend on Thursday.

43
Don't go out on any weeknight when you have a class before 9:30 the next morning.

44
Don't discourage your feelings of homesickness.
They pass.

45
Write – don't call – friends from home.
A return letter is so much better than a phone call.

46
Listen to college radio.
It's a great way to hear music
that's played nowhere else.

47
Read the school paper cover to cover.

48

Read at least the front-page stories of a newspaper every day.

There are papers from all over the country in the library.

49
Don't cheat yourself by using Cliff's Notes.
You'll wish you had read the whole book later.

50
Bring many towels.

51
Put your name in your socks.

52
*Get stamps (a huge supply)
before you leave home.*

53
*Write to your grandparents
every two weeks.*

54
Take baby-sitting jobs when possible.
A family is great to know while away at school.

55

*Keep a jar of peanut butter
stashed away for emergencies.*

56

Always have a dictionary and thesaurus handy.

57

Heartily greet and thank the cafeteria workers.

They'll remember you and slip you extras.

58

Be happy with who you are.

It shows!

59

Make a friend you can hug.

60
Don't be afraid to cry.
Sometimes it helps.

61
*After two years at school,
visit the Career Counseling Office.*

62
*Make sure your adviser
gets to know you and what you need.*
If there's a problem, get a new one.

63

Know that registration for classes is
HELL.

64

*Never forge your adviser's signature
on registration documents.*
The registrar always knows.

65

Learn to use Lotus, Excel, Microsoft Works and Word, WordPerfect, and PageMaker while they are easily accessible.

66

Never turn in someone's old papers.
It defeats the purpose of going to school, and it could get you in big trouble.

67

Always brush your teeth before bed.

68

Learn to fall asleep with the lights on.

69

Learn to negotiate and work out conflicts with roommates.

70
Always be protected.

71
With a roommate, remember your mess is shared with another.

72
Work out a
bathroom-cleaning schedule.

73
Don't borrow anything
without asking.

74

*Return what you borrow
in the same condition.*

75

Go to a park on Sunday mornings.

76

Write as few checks as possible.
An ATM card will work till you have to pay
rent and bills.

77
Don't withdraw more cash
than you can afford to spend.

78
Learn to balance a checkbook.
The more accurate you are
the more generous your parents will be.

79
DON'T BOUNCE CHECKS.

80

Smile at everyone on campus.
People will usually smile back.

81

*Don't apply for credit cards
until your junior year.*

82
*Never, ever
leave your wash unattended.*

83
*Be prepared to change your major
twenty-seven times.*

84
Find a friend with a car
but don't abuse the favor.

85
Never sleep at a frat house.

86

Don't even think about sleeping at a frat house.

87
Never be afraid to ask questions.
Nobody knows anything till they're seniors.

88
Sit in the front of the classroom.

89

If offered any type of on-campus job, take it.

The hours are good, and the work holidays
are usually the same as the university's holidays.

90

Always go to the health service and get a doctor's excuse for missed classes
even when faking.

91
Save money to buy a computer.
Many places offer student rates.

92
Volunteer with
Habitat for Humanity.

93
*If invited to dinner at a
local student's home, never refuse.*
Home cooking and a family atmosphere
are great cures for homesickness.

94
*Write thank-you notes for
everything.*

95

Wait awhile to move off campus.

There's no rush . . . you'll have the rest of your life
to worry about bills.

96

*Don't worry about having a
serious boyfriend your freshman year.*

97

Know that high school, long-distance relationships rarely last through second semester freshman year.

98

Try to meet as many people on your dorm floor as possible.

99

Remember that people should see others only as they are, not only as they look.

Leave the pettiness and cattiness of high school at home.

100

Allow yourself to grow, change, hurt, love, ache, party, learn, and search in order to become the person you are meant to be.

101

WRITE TO YOUR SISTER.